Eating the Sun

a delicious love story

Rachael Ikins

with essay by Phillip Ikins

ISBN 978-1-947653-58-0
Clare Songbirds Publishing House
Eating the Sun © 2019 Rachael Ikins
Cover Art by Rachael Ikins

All Rights Reserved. Clare Songbirds Publishing House retains right to reprint.
Permission to reprint individual poems must be obtained from the author who owns the copyright.

Library of Congress Control Number: 2019938530

Printed in the United States of America
FIRST EDITION

Clare Songbirds Publishing House Mission Statement:
Clare Songbirds Publishing House was established to provide a print forum for the creation of limited edition, fine art from poets and writers, both established and emerging. We strive to reignite and continue a tradition of quality, accessible literary arts to the national and international community of writers, and readers. Chapbook manuscripts are carefully chosen for their ability to propel the expansion of art and ideas in literary form. We provide an accessible way to promote the art of words in order to resonate with, and impact, readers not yet familiar with the siren song of poets and writers. Clare Songbirds Publishing House espouses a singular cultural development where poetry creates community and becomes commonplace in public places.

140 Cottage Street
Auburn, New York 13021
www.claresongbirdspub.com

Contents

In the Beginning
Poem Prologue — 12

Before Spring
Poems My Mother's Cookbook — 15
Memorial — 16
Waiting — 17
Magic — 18

Spring
Poems Spring Solstice — 22
The Performance — 23
About Phillip's Birthday — 24
Cooking — 25
Eating the Sun — 26
Making Stock — 27
Recipes   Best Cuke Soup — 28
    Phillip's Lettuce Soup for Convalescents — 29
    Ginger Cantaloupe Soup — 30
    Cold Cherry Soup — 31

Summer
Poems What You Hear — 44
Just For a Moment — 44
Snapshots, Solstice, Mid-June — 46
On Picking Tomatoes During the Eclipse — 47
Anniversary — 48
The Gardener — 49
First August in the New Place — 50
The Berry Pickers — 51
Food Porn — 52
Recipes   Grilled Peaches with Goat Cheese & Honey — 53
    Stuffed Squash Blossoms — 54
    Wild Berry Freezer Jam — 55

	Johannisbeer Kuechen	56
	Annual Red Freezer Sauce	57
	Saucy Wench Pesto Sauce	58
	Personal Pan Pizzas	59
	Rachael's Rosemary Potato Chips	60
	Phillip's Humane Method for Lobster	61

Autumn

Poems	As Summer Falls Away	67
	Turning Point	68
	Late October	69
	Pumpkin Vines	70
Recipes	Rachael's Woodland Cream Puffball Soup	71
	Fried Puffball Mushrooms	72
	Raquela's Taco-stuffed Zucchini	73
	Rachael's Twist on Sweet Zucchini Bread	74
	Baked Pumpkin Seeds	75

Winter

Poems	Since the End of It	80
	Blizzard Magic	81
	Prelude to Winter	82
	Winter Journeys, Reading Snow	83
	Polar Vortex	84
	The New Year: March	85
	The Thing is Your Life	86
	Latest Winter Night: Moonrise With Dragons	88
	Invocation	89
Recipes	Rachael's Goulash for Convalescents	90
	Rachael's Winter Garden Goulash Casserole	91
	Rachael's Winter Pizza	92
	Rachael's Winter Dip	93
	Crack	95

Love Endures

Poems	Question	100
	Dogs and Dining by Phillip Ikins	102

*Listen to your heart
when he's calling for you.
I don't know where you're going
And I don't know why.
Listen to your heart
Before you tell him goodbye*

        "Listen to Your Heart" by Roxette

*All of me loves all of you
All your curves and all your edges
All your perfect imperfections
I give all of me to all of you,
You're my end and my beginning,
Even when I lose I'm winning*

        "All of Me" by John Legend

The author wishes to thank the following publications for originally printing her work.

"Winter Journeys", "Reading Snow," *Bear Creek Haiku*
"Eating the Sun", *Pangolin Review*
"The Thing is Your Life," *Blood to Ink, indieblu(e) press,* Cephalopress
"The Gardener", *Encore Magazine*
"On Picking Tomatoes During Eclipse", *Synesthesia Review*
"Latest Winter Night: Moonrise with Dragons", *Dragon Poet Review* & *Page and Spine*
"Dawn After Killing Frost", *Shrew*
"August Love", *Fly on the Wall Poetry*
"Waiting", *Transplanted* (Finishing Line Press)
"Since the End of It", *Slideshow in the Woods* (Foothills)
"Invocation", *The Pen Woman Magazine* and *Just Two Girls*

Artwork:
Home from the Sea, The New York State Fair 2015
Morels, *Bear Creek Haiku* and *Shrew*
Shelter, Critics Choice Best in Show OCCC 2014, second place 2014 Fair, cover for Bella Online's literary journal, *Absolute* 2014, and *The Pen Woman Magazine*

What Love Looks Like, Kip Opperman

Special thank you to Gerald Petro for hanging onto the file cabinet that held so many poems when he moved my belongings from my mother's to my house and for saving the poems until I had the sense to go pick them up. This book would not exist without his thoughtfulness.

My heartfelt thanks to Heidi Nightengale and Laura Williams French for taking a chance on this unique manuscript. Special thanks to Laura for being the best editor an author could ever wish for or work with, and for seeing the truth of the story and helping me shape it into a living book.

*For Phillip who held my heart in his hands,
who holds it still*

The Beginning

Think back to the first time you met the love of your life. Was it in a class on campus? Was it an introduction by a mutual friend? A fender bender and insurances exchanged? Someone you grew up with, living next door? I remember my sociology professor lecturing in the class Marriage and Family Relations I took from him. He explained the law of residential propinquity when it comes to the choice of mate. Simply said, most humans tend to find mates close by.

I was about to meet mine, not long after the day of that lecture. I had grown up in the small town of Skaneateles in upstate New York, at the head of a lake by the same name. It was a tiny village when I was a kid with a real 5 & 10 that sold penny candy and cheap rings that turned your skin green, a doctor, a dentist and not much else.

Meanwhile, about thirty-six miles east, or a twenty-five minute drive depending on which route you took and how fast you were going, my husband-to-be was in Liverpool, New York where he had been living and working since he graduated from Syracuse University medical school. Back then, he spent his days as an intern riding the back of an ambulance that was called to bar fights and stabbings. He became one of the most sought-after thoracic surgeons in the world at the height of his career, training the young man who became personal surgeon to the then Shah of Iran, though Phillip was so modest he was the last person to tell you of any achievements.

Uninterested in money-management, haunted by his experiences in the Army during WW II, where he had been awarded both a Purple Heart and the Bronze Star for bravery, he was content to heal those he could, to ease the pain for those for whom it was too late, and to be paid with a box of home-grown tomatoes if that was what a patient had for currency.

He once told me he had wanted to be a surgeon since he was a kid. He recalled at age six, standing in his older sister's rose bed, brandishing a pretend sword. He informed her that he was going to do brain surgery on her husband one day. He never deviated from the conviction that surgery was his destiny. In a bizarre confluence of events, while stationed in Germany during the war, his unit bunked on the floor in a mansion they had taken in battle. As he lay in his bed-roll he stared at a portrait that hung over the cold fireplace. He recognized the face as that of a man named Dr. Ferdinand Ernst Sauerbruch, the founder of modern chest surgery.

My friend Marj had just sat down in my hospital room with a steaming mushroom pizza from Luigi's. My final semester at Syracuse University I had been sick for months. My family practice doctor thought it was only a student virus, but X-rays revealed an object the size of a tennis ball low in my right lung. I spent May-June in a hospital room scribbling poetry, sick to my stomach on the high dose of antibiotics the doctors wished would cure the cyst which is what it turned out to be. That pizza was the first food I'd had appetite for in two weeks.

Just as she opened the box and steam wafted out, a handsome trim man with close-cropped silver hair walked quickly into my room. He hitched one side of his butt over the foot board of my bed and smiled kindly at me as he extended his hand with the words, "Hi. I'm Phillip Ikins. I'm a chest surgeon." My mouth dried right up desiccated as a desert. Images of buzz-saw blades whizzed through my head. Marj closed the pizza box.

I'm sure I shook his hand and introduced her, but all I remember was nausea and the simultaneous, irreverent and perhaps hysterical observation that I kept to myself about how shapely were his thighs. Phillip wore a three-piece, Pierre Cardin, light brown, pin-striped suit and a white shirt. Around his neck draped something I'd never seen, a gold stethoscope. Eventually, I would learn it had his initials engraved on it. How could a person be scared to death and yet notice how handsome somebody was?

After he left, I sent Marj home with the pizza. I wrote a poem about his visit, the image of that stethoscope glinting around his neck. A few days later, I gave it to him. He said, "I love poetry." I thought at the time that he was just being nice.

Saturday July 8, on my late grandfather's birthday, Phillip operated and removed the lobe, a vestigial piece of twin plus cyst. Twins ran on my dad's side of the family. My father had had an extra half kidney. During the operation, the back of his hand rested against my heart. In later years he would brag that he had marked my heart as his. Surgery was uneventful. A week later I was discharged. I went home to stay with my mother until I was well enough to return to my apartment with my dogs and cats in late August. By the time fall semester started, I was back at work and classes.

My last follow-up appointment with Dr. Ikins was in December, right before holiday break. I took time off from work without remembering to let my boss know. I thought I would be in and out, but an hour and a half crawled by. I kept watching other patients go into the inner sanctum. The staff behind the window put their heads together and whispered.

Finally, an older nurse came to get me and when the doctor walked in it wasn't Dr. Ikins. He was performing emergency surgery. I cried all the way the drive back to work totally confused as to why I was crying, got in trouble with my boss, and later phoned my neighbor, Mary, to ask her what she thought was wrong with me. Diagnosis – in love. By the time January rolled around I screwed up my courage to telephone him. He hadn't forgotten me either. And so, our relationship evolved into the love of a lifetime.

Prologue

Spider-small black
Kitten rappelling down
Your shirt and pants leg
Hatting your head in bed

        At night
        Fascinated shoulder-monkey,
        A squeaky toy including himself
        In everything you do, purrs
        Chainsaw loud.

Raised between my breasts and
Floated safe on their islands
One candlelit January bathtub;
Turtlenecked my chin, two smoke-blue eyes
Glistening.

        While he lived with me
        He was you who
        Did not yet and

        Now at your house
        Where I should be (we)

A go-between
Our spirit carrier.

        When you bring him home
        You will at last take root
        With all of us, jungle-dwellers
        Who understand fragile
        Tropical plants.

Before Spring

February is the time of year the seed catalogs arrive. I remember my parents sitting up late at our round kitchen table, heads bent over the pages, making a list of wishes. My father had been forced to weed the family vegetable patch when he was a little boy. This chore so scarred him, it wasn't until he entered his forties that he and my mother began vegetable farming. He bought an ancient John Deere B tractor, a machine so cantankerous it almost drove him nuts. One of the Christmases shortly after they decided to start farming, Dad gifted my mom a weed eater and a canning set. At the time I didn't really understand, and he was at a total loss, as to why when she opened them, she began to cry. A sexy negligee or perfume those gifts were not.

We went to Sears one evening after supper and after much deliberation they chose an upright freezer the size of a full fridge. Before long, and while the snow was still melting, it took up residence in the corner of the cellar where my mom's canning cupboard lived. My dad was by training a mechanical engineer and very methodical in his approach to everything. He attacked the vegetable garden with equal parts methodology and fervor. Dad was trying to start his own manufacturing business during the Carter years and the recession was not a friend to small businessmen. To make a long story short, I would say at least a quarter of our back field became a truck patch. They planted everything from chards to tomatoes, potatoes, peanuts, rhubarb, raspberries, asparagus, corn, beans, and anything else. We ate fresh in season, but as summer progressed, they also spent Saturdays enslaved to the stove blanching and canning.

More esoteric tools showed up like the mandolin type thing with which kernels can be stripped from corn cobs. By November the Sears upright freezer was jam-packed. Since I was a young woman in college and working, I didn't care much, and yet the following February when my mom served a bowl of corn, I was amazed at that just-off-the-cob taste. Their garden fed our family of four all winter and into early spring.

My Mother's Cookbook

Everyone's mother had one,
Fanny Farmer or Irma Rombauer, Julia.
The original queens of the kitchen.
A book that was the go-to even as more exotic volumes joined the shelf.
Stained pages, coffee rings on inside covers.
Notes scribbled, illegible codes.
Recipes in grandma's language nobody is left to translate.
Nuggets of unknown substances sticking chapters forever closed.

Broken-backed, swollen with fifty years of recipes clipped from Good Housekeeping, McCall's, Redbook, years before Cooking Light or Martha Stewart. Stuffed like a turkey.

Dinner parties, birthday bashes, hundreds of weeks of nightly meals first for newlyweds, one then two children. Nieces, nephews. Grandkids. Holiday feasts. Dogs licked roast pans, cats thieved morsels from carving boards. Napkin-wrapped carrots snuck to the horse.

More intimate than a diary, this record of the life of a family.

Nobody touches the book.
Nobody wants it.
The woman managing the sale tags it $2.
Our giggles echo off living room walls,
who would pay $2 for that?

Final day, house sold, movers' truck growled down the drive
we await the trash guy. We pull the last books off shelves and
that cookbook flies lopsided like an overweight bird and splats,
spills on bare hardwood, a liquid sound.
We try not to laugh, feel like crying.

The realtor says, "All things end."
Breaks the spell. We bump heads as we gather papers to our breasts,
fingers scrabble scraps, stuff a garbage bag. Hear the hauler as we straighten up
knot the bag and yes.
All things end.

Memorial

It is the second-best time
of spring, early June
when the poppies and peonies
nod to one another,

blowsy old whores discussing
young men's juices
over a garden gate.

And foxglove regulates
heartbeats of hummingbirds
and platoons of iris stroke their beards,
march through
clouds of phlox perfume
in this small sunlit space
which is all I have
to offer.

Waiting

When I began the long slide
down winter's trough into darkness,
when all the light went,
chill seeped into the bones of my soul.

I forgot.

Spring sunlight pouring through
my east window in a solid yellow
rush, inexorable as spilling paint.

I forgot the tuning symphony
of winds and strings; phoebe, cardinal, the ventriloquist
starling who tries all instruments at once.
Stalking crows, one foot in front of the other,
a bonded pair, blue-black belly-danced intensity.

I remember when they sieved beaks through
January snow for dropped sunflower seeds.
Voles tunneled unseen far

below. Like my love for
you. My heat for you.
Such a surprise, you.
I had forgotten the after-supper walks up the road,
pink-tongued spring sunsets, taking you by the hand
to marvel over sprouting bulbs and buds.
Now, I remember.

Magic

Solemn procession, gray days,
whiteness, black and pricking silver.
Stars, moon. My body craves color
an earthworm excavating darkness.
pepper's red riot
pears' greenish gold curves,
dimpled berries' stain, magenta kisses,
lavish green frills,
lettuces flounced purple.

One rare blue-sky morning,
Sun touches my blind face.
I recall a sense of me after such absence.
Invisible fingers tap-tapping skin.
Nourish my bones.

Spring

I have always loved houseplants. Surrounded by gardeners of all kinds—my mom perennials, my grandmother, who could make a dead stalk of anything bloom, with her cacti, tuberous begonias and roses. My grandfather grew dahlias and my aunt and uncle grew vegetables and flowers. It was guaranteed that the "gene for green" lived in my blood. It was both necessary, and inevitable, that my future spouse share my love of growing things as well as a passion for animals (especially cats).

I married late by contemporary standards. While I finished my college education and worked, I filled my tiny dark apartment with windows bursting with plant life. I hacked a little patch out of chalky hard dirt in front of a neighbor's window for tomatoes. Eventually there were tomato thieves as well, but I let them share. I dug up and planted terrariums with sedums and purslane. My friends laughed at the tall plant I rescued from beneath someone's balcony. It was a magnificent marijuana plant. Who knew?

As I mentioned earlier, my husband and I met during this time early '80s, when he saved my life. He removed an extra piece of lung I was born with, as well as a cyst that had plagued me and caused pneumonia all my life. He performed the surgery the summer of my twenty-seventh birthday. It took him fifty-five minutes. The back of his hand rested against my beating heart as he worked. I wrote him poetry throughout my month-long stay in the hospital. I had written poetry since I was in grade school. I did not know at the time how much he loved poetry. I learned many months or a year later that he had carried one of my poems daily, transferring it with care from suit pocket to another suit pocket. That poem traveled with him to the University of Michigan at Ann Arbor where he showed it to a member of the English department.

Our love bloomed slowly. It took nearly six months after my last post-op visit for us to realize we were destined to be together. The first time he visited my place, one January evening during the symphony intermission, my rescue dog, a half- Pekinese/half-chihuahua, named Pooh, a previously, one-person canine, flopped across Phillip's lap. My heart leaped. Dogs don't lie.

Phillip was fifty-seven when he became my surgeon. I turned twenty-eight that summer of 1982 while in the hospital. Six months after that event, neither of us thought much about the age difference. When you fall in the love the way we did, throwing yourself into it like a sky diver, you feel invincible and immortal.

Right around Valentine's Day, Phillip showed up with some eggs in a pocket, nutmeg, a pint of cream and a hunk of gruyere cheese in another and made me an omelet. His avocation was the creation of French cuisine. He used to say, "I thought all twelve-year-old boys made crepes Suzette for their parents' dinner parties." He had noticed my refrigerator was basically empty. Thankfully nothing was said, my shaky pride more or less intact. I was subsisting at the poverty level as a working student, recovering from major surgery. When we hugged goodbye, he slipped something into the pocket of my robe. After he was gone, I pulled out a hundred-dollar bill. Unsure whether to be hurt or angry, in confusion I phoned him. To my question, "Why?" He simply said, "I know what it is to be hungry." I went grocery shopping. I spent $98.00.

January 23, 1987, on his birthday, Phillip and I married in our living room. The fireplace was burning, the finches and canaries in the flight cage made sweet music with their songs and Pooh, in his pink-striped bow-tie borrowed from Daddy (the dog who'd lain across Phillip's lap that first visit) sat on the train of my wedding gown throughout the ceremony. I wore my mother's dress from 1945. My mother was an artist and my father a pilot, she designed the gown which was made in from the silk of my father's parachute.

photo courtesy Peter J. Wittkuhns © 1987

Spring Solstice

Mud's swollen tongue
licks slow strokes on my rubber
boot seams. Spring run-off,
Melting snow pools like juice
of a woman's plump folds.

Above my head, feathers in flocks
stroke air and the sky sighs.

The Performance

The trees rustle, shift in their seats.
Programs rattle. A few cough.
Wind rushes through the rafters, this sky-bowl
auditorium,

The Show. We wait for the Show to begin.
In the apple orchard on the hill,
young trees crabbed by snow raise reddening fingers
to sun. Stretch, scrawl a message, red letters on blue.
Then the birds.

About Phillip's Birthday

I skated by the lower pond,
From my hill-high perch, the gelling ice,
an alien hand, starfish-fingered
sweated into the surface,
a commemoration.

The birthday sign I painted
celebrates from the barn door,
Three deflating balloons, the blue one
almost full even under such snow and cold.

Consider it, that container of air, my breath and
Kisses, words, laughter, a hollow sphere full.
That moment when
I inhaled
and you were born.

Cooking

He brought a bouquet
of orchids for my kitchen sill.
Consider their parts.
My hand strokes, seasons
this tenderloin.

Also, two
warmed rounds of
bread, nestled in a basket,
soft towel tucked whitely between
brown skins.

Strong.
Baker's hands.
He says,
"Let me give you these."

Eating the Sun

Cheeks against your own
alive with warmth. So real you expect
what you hold to twist in your hand
like a kitten or a baby.

It doesn't matter whether it is cobbed corn
swaddled in layers of silk and green.
Tomatoes, potatoes disturbed from the sleeping
Earth. Heat permeates.

As you preheat the oven or wait for the steamer to boil
your fingers quest for it again and again,
and your face wants that warm-blood humming against
your skin. It tumbles from your fingers

into pot, baking pan, the oven door
bangs shut, you think,
"I eat the sun."

Making Stock

When Phillip taught me how to make stocks it was an eye opening experience. No watery faint-flavored chicken blandness that I grew up with.

One late summer, after we bought our house, in part because of the enormous cooking fireplace in the basement complete with wrought iron hook from which to hang a big pot, we started with the basic ingredients and cooked the whole batch in that fireplace, then reserved some of various kinds, beef, chicken and vegetable to reduce to brown sauce and ultimately Demi-glacé sauce. This "liquid gold" as he termed it, was stored in small amounts in freezer bags and shared through the winter when he made his specialties, tournedos Rossini and Beef Wellington. He made the latter starting with from-scratch puff pastry crust.

For chicken stock he would add to his enormous stock pot a cookie sheet full of broiled chicken wings, and turkey parts, giblets and wings. Chicken carcasses from roast whole chicken. We set the pot which could not hang over the open flames on a metal grilling stand. For beef he would add to the chicken wings, ribs and beef soup bones that had been grilled in the oven. Water and carrots, celery, onion. That particular early autumn we made the fireplace stock, we kept the fire going 48 hours non-stop. One of us was always home or awake tending it. The wood smoke lent that batch, which was probably the best he ever made, an exquisite flavor.

After it had cooked down he'd strain all the bones and carcass and poured the liquid back into the pot. If he was making beef stock, Phillip poured a bottle of good red wine such as a Bordeaux to the pot. If it was a chicken stock, white wine. He added fresh cut bunches of garden herbs of choice, preferring huge amounts of lovage, chives, cilantro, and so forth. His favorite for poultry was French tarragon. Depending on what kind of sauce, and for which dish he wanted to end up with, the time for continuing to cook and reduction varied.

Best Cuke Soup
Adapted from Allrecipes.com

1-2 whole cucumbers
4 c chicken stock
(*My preference is to make my own stock using a whole barbecued chicken carcass. Cook it in 2 quarts of water and add fresh herbs i.e. Rosemary, thyme, parsley or whatever you prefer. An onion, carrots if desired. Add a bottle of beer or a cup of white wine. Simmer.*)

2 Tbsp chopped onion or scallions
2 Tbsp butter
fresh French Tarragon
fresh parsley
2 Tbsp plain yogurt or sour cream

Peel and seed the cucumber and put in blender or food processor and liquify. Add stock to cucumber in blender. Sauté the chopped onions or scallions until soft but not caramelized in the butter. Salt to taste. *I like to use sea salt.* Chop one bunch of French tarragon and parsley until minced very finely. Add to blender and blend. Combine with 2 large Tbsp plain yogurt or sour cream before serving. May be eaten hot or cold.

Will not freeze.

Phillip's Lettuce Soup for Convalescents

1 C. chicken stock
1 C. sweet leaf lettuce
1 Tbsp yogurt or sour cream
Salt to taste

Tear the lettuce leaves. Simmer the stock. Add lettuce. Cook a few minutes but don't overcook them. Remove from heat and stir in the yogurt. Serve with toast or crackers.

Garden fact: Each strand of corn silk corresponds to one kernel of corn. Each strand must be individually fertilized by bees and wind. If you get a cob with gaps, that means fertilization was not complete.

Ginger Cantaloupe Soup
Adapted from Joy of Cooking

1 medium-large ripe cantaloupe
1 C. orange juice
2 Tbsp lemon juice
¼ C. lime juice
½ C. ginger (*either fresh or jarred ginger peeled, and minced fine*)
fresh mint leaves and berries for garnish

Cut up and peel the melon and add chunks to food processor or blender. Process until smooth. Add orange, lemon, and lime juice. Process to combine well. *If using fresh ginger, peel and mince fine. Also can use minced ginger.* With your hand squeeze the juice from ½ cup minced ginger into a small bowl. Take 2 Tbsp of the juice and add to blender. Serve chilled with fresh mint garnish and berries of choice.

Cold Cherry Soup
Adapted from Joy of Cooking

2 lbs. cherries. (*I used Bing cherries, pitted and halved.*)
2 cups Gewürztraminer or medium dry white wine
2 cups water
¼ cup sugar
4 tsp cornstarch
1 tsp grated orange zest
1 Tbsp fresh orange juice
1 Tbsp fresh lemon juice
1 Tbsp plain yogurt or sour cream
fresh mint

Reserve half the cherries and place the other half in a soup pot with wine and water. Bring to a boil. Reduce heat and simmer until cherries are softened (about 15 minutes). Purée in processor or blender.
In a small bowl combine sugar and cornstarch. Add 3 Tbsp purée to cornstarch mixture and stir well. Return paste to pot and cook on high heat, whisking until thickened, about 5 minutes. Reduce heat and stir in reserved cherries with orange zest, orange juice, and lemon juice. Simmer until heated through. Adjust sweetness with sugar and lemon juice. Serve hot or cold garnished with sour cream or plain yogurt and mint sprigs from the garden.

photo courtesy of Joseph T. Hubbard © 1955

Summer

We bought our first house in 1984. The back yard must have once been a terraced garden but now was shaded by many big trees. We planted shade-loving perennials and fenced it in for our dogs. We concentrated our mutual love of gardening on the front yard. Phillip built barriers for up to seven compost piles. One of his favorite books was titled *Let It Rot*. My dad's style of composting had been to dump wagon loads of grass clippings along with my mother's perennial refuse into the hedgerow and dig some out to mulch the tomato rows. Phillip's composting, where we saved kitchen scraps and gave back to the earth from our kitchen appealed to my poet's heart.

Before long, the barren front yard of our little stone cottage-style house was filled with roses, crabapple trees, and currant bushes from which we made a German dessert Johannisbeer Kuchen. I rooted a pussy willow cutting from a tree at my childhood home, and we planted it. Herbs of all sorts were a novelty for me. As a chef who favored French cuisine, Phillip knew their value and introduced me to such rarities as sorrel which sprouted earliest in spring, lovage – a relative of celery, French tarragon and more. Garlic and leeks walked our beds. We halved our driveway by building a retaining wall, which allowed extra sun space for more plants. I put so many daffodils in our yard it became a sea of yellow every April. We tore down the garage and replaced it with a solarium. The end of the driveway closest to the house became a corn plot with a dump truck-load of reprocessed top soil from the sewage treatment facility. From Onondaga County, we picked up a coffee can of red wigglers and started a worm farm in a recycling bin in an artificially lit greenhouse we crafted from old storm windows. We also used it for February seedlings and orchids. Phillip, like my Opa, raised dahlias. And like Oma, he had a passion for roses.

We learned, either from a friend or in the newspaper, that the city mulch pile was not far from us. Frequently after spreading reeking compost, we'd jump into our Subaru Brat and head to the mulch pile with a box of big black trash bags, a shovel and a pitchfork. We unloaded our bursting bags over the half-decomposed compost. Usually that dimmed the fragrance. Neighbors never complained. With each of the twenty plus years we worked that earth we enriched it.

When Phillip was still in practice, he saw patients daily during office hours and at all the local hospitals and would drive up to hundred miles to perform surgeries when necessary. We wanted to be together every minute, so we had a special code for me to phone his beeper. When he saw the code, he knew I was thinking of him and would call me when he had a break. I made his lunch every day and stood on the stoop or in the driveway after one last hug and lingering kiss and waved until his Jeep was out of sight.

Some afternoons he would swing by to pick me up. I would wait with a book while he visited patients on rounds. Petrushka, our Newfoundland/Labrador mix, became Daddy's girl and his best traveling companion. If the beeper went off in the night, she squealed with pleasure, bounced wagging back and forth while he phoned in. If he hung up and went back to bed, she threw herself back on her bed with a gusty, depressed groan.

She saved him one hot summer at 2 a.m., while they waited stopped at a light in a rough part of town, a man materialized out of the shadows swinging a heavy chain to smash the windshield. Luckily, the window on the passenger side was rolled down so 'Trushka could enjoy the night breeze. She roared out of it, this huge black dog with a snarling mouth of long white teeth gleaming in the dark; the guy dropped his weapon and ran.

We counted the days until his retirement and after Phillip retired one of his favorite outdoor art projects involved us driving around town to collect old wooden pallets. He took them apart and then cut designs and rebuilt them to make ornamental fences and gates for the backyard compost areas. We also rescued a massive cross section of a fabulous maple tree from somebody's driveway pile. Using fence posts for legs, we crafted a burl table to stand with cedar chairs under the rose trellis we had constructed as a living car port. We cooked outside, almost every day, even in snow. Countless meals graced that table.

The original owner of the house was amazed at how things grew as they could get "nothing to grow." During our renovations of the house we discovered that if we dug a foot down the soil was littered with the fieldstone rubble from the construction of the house. Of course, nothing grew, the soil pH being too alkaline from the stone debris.

We eventually added on a second solarium. Loving the paradox of a stone house with glass rooms, we read up on water gardens. The summer of the hot tub we designed a garden lily pool which was a delight to photograph from the heights. Paths of flat stones or mulch meandered through our lush flowers.

When it became necessary to have a new roof installed, an unexpected surprise was revealed. Our house looked like a salt-box style Cape Cod from the front with steep roof. But there was an almost-flat section over the guest bedroom. We asked our roofers if they could design a hatch with drop-down attic-type ladder there so that we could access the sunny space. An added railing and then a layer of indoor-outdoor carpet created a comfortable place for our telescope, picnics, and birdwatching. We planted sun-loving vegetables like eggplant along the railing and seeded a cold frame, made from old wood and a glass storm window, with marigolds, zinnias, lettuces and other annuals. We screwed multiple hoses together, dragged through the house, tied one end to the roof garden's railing then dropped the other end down the roof to screw onto the outdoor faucet. Thus, water up top. I always wanted to sleep out there on hot summer nights, but we never did. The dogs braved the ladder and of course, the cats loved everything about it.

Our tuxedo boy, Gaucho, managed to catch a fledgling crow which was as big as he was. He zipped in the front door, through the house. We cornered him and were able to get the baby bird from him. No blood. The crow family was hysterical outside. We clambered up the ladder with excited dogs and birds screaming. Carefully Phillip inched along the roof peak that jutted off our flat garden. He set the baby on the shingles as the parents dive-bombed his head. They fell silent, finally figuring out that we were helpers. The baby flew off, and we gathered all the kitties inside for the night. Subsequent afternoons I enjoyed reading on the roof, watching the flight lessons as the baby plopped into the hedge while anxious flock mates cawed directions. Phillip always said, "that bird will never earn his pilot's license."

I saved some feeder goldfish, comets destined to be dinner for my turtles and my large Oscar, Aylseworth (after one of Phillip's patients) who lived on top of Phillip's antique player piano and released them into our pool. Birds, squirrels, and raccoons visited our many feeders and enjoyed the fountain, attracted by the sound of the water. A bullfrog found his way to our oasis somehow, in the middle of the city.

We tried to sculpt a three-tier fountain from directions in a garden magazine, in a cement mixing pan with perlite, concrete mix and vermiculite. It never held water, but it was very enjoyable to mix the mucky media together. Phillip named it the "elephant turd." We planted perennials in the "cups."

After our first winter dwindled and spring thawed the pool, I sat outdoors one sunny afternoon and stared into the water. I saw a fingernail-sized fry. The comets had multiplied. After a number of years, that little pool became more orange than not, it held so many piscine inhabitants. When winter waned, the cats stalked impatiently on the ice, peering at the fish. Certain cats learned to be great fishers.

We loved each other's company and did everything together, bathing, cooking, hiking, biking, gardening and reading. While other people complained when a spouse was suddenly at home every day, we

Rachael Ikins © 1985

Rachael Ikins © 1988

couldn't wait. When he retired from his profession as a thoracic surgeon and award-winning teacher of surgery in 1994, one of the first things he did was go to the Apple store to buy his first lap-top.

Winters we worked long days as he learned the computer and transcribed poem after poem from my hundreds of notebooks onto floppy disks. He printed multiple copies of each one and put them in folders in an elaborate catalogue system which corresponded to the series of disks he had burned. From there he set about trying to find a literary agent, and he also helped me submit to countless journals. While he did all of that, I wrote and revised.

After eight wonderful years, we began to face a series of challenges. We struggled with both health and financial issues. Phillip was fifty-seven and I, twenty-seven when we met. Because we loved each other "au coup de foudre" as the French say, we did not notice our age difference, nor did we care. Age is no guarantee of anything.

Phillip quietly retired at sixty-five without fanfare, no party and without telling his associates or staff. A few short months later, he suffered his first heart attack. Eventually, he would have three heart attacks, culminating in quadruple bypass surgery, but by then his heart was so scarred he was never quite himself again and lived with worsening heart failure for the rest of his life.

I struggled with mental health issues that required a plethora of medications. These caused a series of adverse reactions and damaging side effects. By 1998, I was able to wean off of all the prescription medications, but I almost died in the process. A year later, while Phillip was in his urologist's office receiving the news that his prostate cancer was not responding to treatment, I had a miscarriage. I was forty-seven.

That night, we went to bed right after supper, the windows were open, and the warm sweet spring air flowed in. We held each other and cried ourselves to sleep.

Neither of us was able to manage finances well during so much illness. So, by the time I was off the medications, Phillip's pension was all but gone. Forced to downsize, we moved from the home and garden where we had married and created so much together, and declared bankruptcy. We ended up in a tiny ramshackle house clinging to the side of a mountain in a small town east of Syracuse. One night I dreamt we had snuck back home while the new owners slept. Parked our car in our beloved garden and filled the green garden cart with plants. I felt so relieved. Then, I woke up.

Due to the higher elevation, winters in Erieville were especially harsh. January 2004, I was spreading newspaper by the back door to help absorb snow-melt we and the dogs tracked in and saw an ad for a poetry contest put on by the local chapter of the National League of American Pen Women in conjunction with the *Syracuse Post Standard*. I tore it out of the paper. I was fifty-two and had all but given up my dream of being a professional writer. I had never received family support for my writing until I married Phillip, even though I had the occasional journal acceptance in my late teens and early twenties.

I chose a few poems to submit, printed them, and yanked on tall boots to trudge through a blizzard to leave the entry in our mailbox. Weeks passed. The phone rang in early March. Phillip called me into the house.

"It's the Pen Women contest person." He said. "They wondered if you could send the entry fee."

I had no experience with such things and had not known from the newspaper blurb that there was one. Luckily, it was only three dollars and I mailed it out the next day.

Spring began to creep out of the frozen earth, called forth by the lengthening sunlight. We ventured down to our pond too, marveling at the renaissance of nature around us that started to have a healing effect on us both.

One evening our pig, Roosevelt, and I walked to the mailbox after supper while Phillip washed dishes. I pulled out an envelope marked NLAPW.

"Oh, shit," I said to Roosevelt who grunted back at me. "What do they want *now?* "

I knew better than to dare hope for even an honorable mention. I tore open the envelope. Inside the letter stated: "Congratulations. Your poem "Winter Chorus" has won first prize and "Girlie" an HM." Both poems were later published in my debut chapbook *Slide-show in the Woods* (2008, Foothills.) I looked behind me to see to whom the letter was referring and then down at Roosevelt. My heart pounded.

"What is HM?"

Then the letter's message sank in. I started to run in those big clunky rubber boots up the muddy driveway, past the sprouting peonies and the Rose of Sharon we had been able to grab from our old garden when we moved. I slammed into the back door out of breath. Phillip turned to look at me with concern, his hands in soapy water. My chest was heaving. "I won first prize!!!!" I was finally able to gasp, "An Honorable Mention."

We stood in the sunset of that late March evening holding each other tight, each of us crying into the other's shoulder. He gave me a ring one Christmas that said "Two bodies, one heart." When we held each other, my chin fit exactly into the hollow of his collarbone. We were a matched set, a lone pair surviving a difficult journey.

Rachael Ikins © 2005

What You Hear

At 2 a.m. when you aren't
listening for your heart to beat;

Bullfrog's lovesick groan from
the pond. Tomcat calling the perimeter
as he hugs the shrubs
for the catnip he thinks you planted
for him.

Something wild that cries like a human baby—
grief or death or mating lust?
The dogs lift their heads to the window.

You don't hear your heart or feel it speed up as you wonder
is that cry a newborn fawn? Or that sad little mop of a dog Molly
who was barking desperation when you fell asleep?
Her owner leaves her out hours in all weathers.

But the dogs slump back into blankets.
Wind's hand riffles Solstice. Sudden lushness of leaves.
And you find yourself eyes wide open
looking out the window for June's first fireflies
stunned wakeful by the storm of silence
in your chest.

Home From the Sea © 2015 Rachael Ikins

Just for a Moment

this mid-June morning
I stand in my garden, watering.
Wearing sleep shorts and an old tee shirt,
bareheaded without sun screen or
bug repellent or my special sunglasses.

Just for a moment I don't think about
people who laugh at the notion of saving money by
growing my own food and how when you add
cost of bags of soil and mulch and the water bill
my heirloom vegetables cost more than at the big box
supermarket. I don't care. I compost.

I don't care, in this suspended time warp,
about the hole in the ozone layer, or the two basal cell carcinomas they
removed from my nose and eye socket,
legacy of a childhood burn that took even my finger and toenails.
Just for a minute, I let myself love the warm hand of the sun
caressing my neck. The way the earth softens after watering, a
cushion for bare feet. I'll risk the ticks.

Humans assume that all the earth has to offer
is ours, and no other life form deserves respect or equality. Our need
trumps all so yank it out, cut it down, poison it, shoot it,
asphalt over it and so forth. I saw a clip online of a herd of bulldozers
crunching the last trees in a certain jungle, a lone orangutan screamed,
clinging to his tree
as the blade took it.

Just for a moment, there are the finches at the feeder in their
purple coats, squirrels tiptoeing along the new fence pickets and
mysterious woods-birds' songs calling me back to childhood. Maybe
they are fairies. The wren I named 'Henry' who lives behind my house
chortling all day. The dogs flopped on the deck as I watch an orange
moth, disturbed by hose spray flutter to a drier perch.

I think about the spinach, lettuce and radishes I picked yesterday,
a salad for lunch. I wonder—have the nutrients they pulled from this
earth combined in my cells yet. I wonder if the organisms in the earth
have absorbed the redolent gasp of compost, all winter's kitchen scraps
that I gave back.

Just for a moment there is a cosmic finger on the "pause" button,
I am again only a barefoot girl in sleep shorts watering her vegetable
garden sun's arm around my shoulders, droplets splashing my legs.

Snapshots, Solstice, Mid-June

Swelling moon silvers poplar trees.
Leaves shiver, fireflies spark
code, shooting ground-stars that burst
pulled toward that shining face.
Polaris beams and for a moment I think
it is a fire, floating skyward.

Dawn blushes the cooled morning cloud-
bellies, breezes wash poplar hands. A song of hush
lifts my hair off my neck. Then the babies.
Grackle parents mobbed by shrieking twins,
robins leading broken-winged chicks
to peck the grass for worms.
Cardinal babies' wind-chime
call begging for food. A male splashes redness almost
stains my hand where I sip coffee on the balcony
teaches his offspring to fly.

All of it, moon's reflection in sidewalk puddles,
birds, and trees hostage to humans who gobble the planet.
I read while drinking my cardinal-blessed coffee that in
600 years there will be
no more trees.

On Picking Tomatoes During the Eclipse

Sky holds its breath.
White light, no birdsong
nor crickets.

Shadows stamp
the lawn ahead of me.
My heart flutters,
a moth trapped
in leaves. My hackles
rise, static crackles toward
the moon.

I kneel to pick tomatoes
during the eclipse.
Keep my eyes to the ground
fingering red globes.

I tumble them into my shirt,
limp toward the house
juggling my load.

Hours after, the moon races south.
Katydids question. I reach for
tomatoes to make sauce to freeze.
Touch life, gravid with heat,
fruit soaked with friction of moon-and-sun
against my cheek, my ear listening for
a heart beat.
I pour the last cups
into freezer bags,
label them "eclipse."

Anniversary

After the day,
after the supper,
candles light.
You carried my boots, me
so far.

We slip front to front
underwater, not one drop gleams
between, we are that close.
Fragrant oil-sheened.

After 25 years, my spoonie-chin
fits into your collar bone's bowl.
My arms encircle your chest just
to there, where my fingers lie like minnows,
at home in the troughs your ribs create.
We breathe.

In deeper water fish investigates weed-tangle.
Some tongue licks lips.
Somewhere, an inhalation.
You-and-me.

Under cats and covers,
Night's darkest secret,
I whisper in your ear and
you slide, slide home.

The Gardener

Insistent sounds of motor bikes which play
Within the field, pull my attention from
The book upon my lap, and I go gaze,
Annoyed at the boy-riders under sun's last rays.

The blonde-haired boy said "Hi" to me this morning,
"See ya" with a blonde-haired nod as he rode
By me, while I bent red-faced over some
Forget-me-nots and daisies by the road.

And motor-bike purr makes me think of you;
It makes me wonder what you did today.
Your voice can vibrate like that motor's tune
Through your bones, shoes, to the floor, all the way
To the chair where I sit absorb, and melt.
Into your shadow, I shall always stay in love; yours.

First August in the New Place

First at-home with vegetable garden
rioting below the studio window.
Pumpkins and zucchini levitate
like some square alien craft that hovers to spy.
We've lived here 9 mos.
Already death has touched us twice,

as death drove us out last summer
to root somewhere
or die.

Cicada choir chants the sun up.
Katydid rasp pulls it down.
Pastes the moon in its place,
riding silver clouds,
meteors pricking through.

It was always August.
Just when summer comes into its own;
I think it will last forever.
My favorite month
begins
the slow good bye.

The Berry Pickers

Late insect-singing
summer and
raspberries drip
on their vines.

Wild grapes
cluster with bird-
flocks among
those cherry trees
in the second hedgerow.

My lips are stained
scarlet and purple
with passionate
Sunday's juices.

When you come
tomorrow, lovey,
don't forget
a basket for collecting.
We will freeze these
sweat-dewed fruits
to bake pies midwinter.

My breasts want
for your palm's skin
to gather them in.

Food Porn

Grilled peaches' heat melts
goat cheese stuffing, drizzled
honey, a dash of cinnamon.
Silken tofu spun with
semi-sweet morsel melt,
liquid lusciousness.
Blender chocolate mousse.

Unhusked corn ears
across hot charcoal.
Outer leaves crisped curl,
striped black, pale as paper.
Sweetness, butter, melting down the chin.

Prosciutto's opal translucence
rolled around cream cheese, a side
of pickles' kiss, eyes water,
and cherries stain fingers,
lips a purple that lingers.
Ice cubes stack a glass,
Shot of seltzer, pink lemonade
trickled like snow-melt. Or
cola with floating lime grin.

Avocados' smiling cream, one sprouted pit, a free tree fingers
July sunlight. mushrooms sautéed
brown/blackness, crackle on the tongue, tenderloin juices, filet as pink
as sunset summer sky.

Black raspberries blue pickers'
hands, lips, red stripes ripped into leg skin.
Freezer jam, nine jars stored in a row.
Containers of pure summer idle to savor
all the dark winter months.
one August delectable at a time.

Grilled Peaches with Goat Cheese and Honey

2 whole peaches
2 Tbsp butter (if cooking in pan)
4 Tsp goat cheese
4 Tbsp honey
cinnamon
mint leaves

Cut fruit in half and remove pits.
If using the grill outdoors, lay peach halves cut side down on grill. If using a sauté pan, melt some margarine or butter and lay halves face down. Cook for several minutes, then gently turn over and grill remaining side until fruit is heated through. While still hot, fill opening where pit was with a teaspoon of goat cheese. Drizzle with local honey. A dash of cinnamon. Garnish with mint leaves and enjoy.

serves 4

The honeybee is now on the endangered species list due to global warming and other factors. We are dependent on bees for the majority of our fruits and vegetables. If you have space in your back yard, don't mow an area. Instead of poisoning with weed killer, allow native species such as clovers and alfalfas to grow. They are an essential part of soil health as they fix nitrogen in the earth which is the main building block in all plants. Many of these are low growing ground covers. Clover has an intoxicating sweet fragrance when it is in bloom. Leaving these ensures a food source for bees and butterflies and prevents soil erosion as well.

Stuffed Squash Blossoms

6 large male blossoms *Any squash blossom will do, including pumpkin flowers.*
1 egg
⅔ C breadcrumbs
1 Tbsp flour
¼ C shredded mozzarella
fresh herbs of choice
¼ C vegetable oil
salsa
sour cream

In 3 separate bowls have one each of whisked egg, breadcrumbs with flour, and a mixture of shredded mozzarella and fresh chopped herbs such as parsley, basil, thyme and rosemary.

Heat a skillet with several Tbsp of oil.

Carefully fill each flower with the cheese/herb mixture. Twist the petals shut and dredge flower first through egg, coating well then the breadcrumbs. Gently lay the coated blossom in the hot oil. Cook for several minutes until you see cheese melting. With small tongs or a soft spatula turn them over until evenly browned on both sides. Remove from heat onto a bed of paper towels. Serve immediately with a side of tomato salsa and a dab of lite sour cream.

Make sure to leave enough male blossoms to fertilize the females so there are squash. It's possible to be so enthusiastic for these succulent treats that you over-pick.

Wild Berry Freezer Jam
From FreshPreserving.com

Whether you go wild berry picking in a park or field or raise berries in your own garden, jam midwinter is a sweet treat. This is delicious no-cook jam.

For every 2 (8oz) half pints of jam you need:
1 2/3 C of berries
1 Tbsp lemon juice
2 Tbsp Instant Pectin
2/3 C granulated sugar *or a no calorie sweetener if preferred.*

Stir sugar and pectin in bowl. (Remember to use instant pectin, not traditional pectin). Add fruit. Stir for 3 minutes. Ladle jam into clean freezer jars and let stand 30 minutes before putting in freezer. Enjoy.

Don't exceed 6 jars of jam per batch. Set may not happen in larger batch sizes.

Johannisbeer Kuechen (currant tart)
Crust recipe adapted from Joy of Cooking

2 C fresh currants
Sugar to taste

½ C unsalted butter
1 egg yolk
1 ¼ C all-purpose flour
½ C sugar
1 tsp grated lemon zest
¼ tsp salt

For a 9 ½-10 inch tart shell

Combine in a bowl or food processor for 10 seconds the flour, ½ C sugar, lemon zest, and salt. Add butter (cut into pieces) Mash with fork or process until mixture resembles coarse crumbs. Add egg yolk. Mix until dough forms a ball. If it is too sticky, refrigerate for 30 minutes. Grease the tart pan, dust with flour and tap out excess. Pat dough evenly over the bottom and up the sides of the pan. Thoroughly prick with a fork. Refrigerate for 30 mins. Preheat oven to 400° F.

From the garden use fresh currants. Carefully remove all stems. Combine currants with sugar to your taste. *Currants are quite tart so everyone's preference may vary.* Bake for 25 mins until crust edges are a golden brown and the currant mixture is bubbling. Serve warm or cold with a dollop of plain or vanilla yogurt or lite sour cream.

Annual Red Freezer Sauce

Depending on how much you want to make, decide for yourself amounts of the following fresh ingredients.

Chopped whole tomatoes (skins on)
Garlic clove
Onion
Fresh herbs of choice (basil, rosemary, thyme, or oregano)
Sweet peppers (Hungarian or banana peppers work great)
Salt

Into a blender or food processor combine tomatoes, garlic clove, onion, herbs. If using oregano, do so sparingly. Add peppers and salt to taste. Blend well. Fill freezer bags. May be used as a basis for spaghetti sauce, pizza sauce, and tomato soup. After defrosting cook it down to the desired consistency. You can also shred zucchini and stir in.

The carbon atom is the basis for all living things. I am made up of carbon atoms. The vegetables in my garden, radishes, spinach, snow peas, corn, pumpkins and so on, all carbon atoms. As I eat these, so do I literally rise up from the Earth herself, a transfer of carbon in one form to another when the fertilized egg's heart begins to sing. When I am an old woman, gravity will pull at my skin, my muscles and my veins will drift toward the surface of thinning skin, parchment skin like an onion's. Carbon calling to carbon and as I rose up from the loam so will my body dissolve back into it. Even clouds of sugar around stars in outer space contain carbon. I belong to the Earth. I am Hers. She made me and fed me and when it is time She will take me back into Herself, my life having been a brief blink when She lent me a soul.

Saucy Wench Pesto Sauce
Based on Joy of Cooking

I always plant a lot of basil. No doubt about it, the taste and intensity of fresh herbs will break you of a salt addiction and makes summer cooking from the garden a healthy and delightful shock to the tongue.

2 cups loosely packed basil leaves
½ C grated Parmesan or Romano. Can add shaved as well.
⅓ C pine nuts*.
2 medium cloves of garlic peeled. **
½ c olive oil

To the blender or processor add the basil, cheese, nuts and garlic. With blender running slowly pour in olive oil and adjust as needed for consistency. The end result should be a fairly thick paste. Salt and pepper to taste.

This sauce will freeze for up to 3 months. If you do that, add the cheeses and nuts after thawing. Store it in the fridge with a light film of olive oil in a tightly sealed container. It will discolor.

*I use walnuts. Alternates are almonds or hazelnuts the latter two requiring more oil.

**I like to grow Egyptian walking garlic. The flower heads remind me of storks and the flavor is great.

Personal Pan Pizzas:
One Dish Delights from the Garden

Naan, pita, or other flatbread
Red Sauce or Pesto*
fresh tomatoes
basil (if using red sauce)
toppings of choice
½ C mozzarella
Parmesan
red pepper

Preheat oven to 425°F
Spray a pizza or cooking sheet with non stick spray.

Start with a Naan, pita, or other flat bread. *If you are very ambitious you can make your own dough in a bread machine or buy ready made dough.*

First spread about ¼ inch sauces. Next layer some sliced fresh tomatoes. Layer basil leaves if using red sauce. You can continue with the toppings of your preference. Mushrooms, olives, banana or Hungarian peppers. Ground sautéed meat of your choice if desired. The final layer should be a heaping handful of shredded mozzarella. I sprinkle some Parmesan and crushed red pepper right before popping the whole confection in the oven.

Bake for 25 minutes until cheese is a golden brown.

*Either Saucy Wench Pesto Sauce or Annual Freezer Sauce work great.

Rachael's Rosemary Potato Chips
Made with fresh dug Kennebec potatoes.

Potatoes
olive oil
cooking spray
sea salt
chopped fresh rosemary

Preheat the oven to 425°F.
Spray a cookie sheet with a non stick spray. Leaving the skins on, slice each potato as thinly as possible. Spread the slices in one layer on the baking sheet. Drizzle olive oil lightly over the exposed flesh. Sprinkle with sea salt and chopped fresh rosemary. Bake for 10 mins. Turn the slices over. Continue baking while watching until the desired color is reached. Chips should be thin and crispy.

Garden fact: As a bee collects pollen from the flower of the oregano plant, the blossom releases an oil which rubs into the bee and kills mites and other parasites in her fur.

Phillip's Humane Method for Sweet, Tender Lobster

Start with several live lobsters.

Put them in a stock pot. Pour in a bottle or two of cold beer. Add enough cold water to cover them. Add fresh cut herbs such as lovage, dill, chives, parsley, whatever your choice.

Set on medium heat and bring slowly to a boil. Once their shells are bright red remove lobsters with tongs. Immediately cut open the shells with sharp shears while they are still hot and soft.

Serve with melted butter or sauce of your choice. Cooking the lobsters in this way anesthetizes them with the alcohol thus relaxing their muscles. The meat is much more tender than muscles which go into rigid shock when an animal is suddenly dumped into boiling water. Save the pot liquor after to make fish stock.

This method utilizing beer (or white wine) also works well for steaming live clams. Same result much more tender meat.

Autumn

No writing about my husband and me would be complete without a section on mushrooms. We spent a lot of time walking in the woods. Both of us found solace in the natural world. We discovered a mutual fascination in mushrooms. Whether as possible sign of faeries in the vicinity or simply because of their bizarre beauty, we would point out new finds to each other wherever we hiked.

I was raised, living eight weeks of every summer at our family camp which included sixty acres of woods and fields. One of the first places I brought Phillip was to those woods. My grandfather bought the land in the 1940s for $1500. Each summer he added on more rooms and buildings with the help of "camp boys," teens from their hometown in NJ who had the best deal: work in the morning, play all afternoon.

My parents were birdwatchers and owned *Peterson's Guide*. Nobody had any other identification books except for one beautiful, coffee table-sized volume illustrated in watercolor plates that belonged to my grandfather about mushrooms. However, parental rule across the board was "if you don't know what it is don't eat it." Just to add emphasis my mom told us many things were poisonous that I've since learned are not. It worked though and kept us safe.

My grandmother did oblige me by making "Haycorn Pancakes" the year I turned eight and read the *Winnie the Pooh* series. I don't remember anything she might have added, except crushed acorns and flour and the sight of the pancakes cooking. Afterward, we set the finished delicacies in the woods for wild animals to eat on a special stump. When we lived with Roosevelt pig in Erieville, I did find out that acorns are poisonous to pigs.

We hunted for wild treasure as children—acorns, snail shells, bird feathers, lucky stones, but mushrooms and toadstools were royalty. I was pleasantly surprised to discover that Phillip liked them, too. He knew quite a bit of their history because of his love of cooking.

Among the classic French delicacies my husband created were duxelles, a form of sautéed down mushrooms which can be the basis for a brown sauce or used in place of truffles. It was inevitable that when he retired, in addition to tackling my poetry, he asked a friend for a used microscope, slides and dyes. We had amassed quite the library of mushroom identification volumes. With the new equipment, the fungi we brought home from our walks in many local natural areas could be stained, and spore prints viewed. Even so, Phillip was so careful that the few times he ate something, he used only himself as a guinea pig. Until, that is, we found morels.

These oddballs look to me sort of like brains on a stalk. They are impossible to mistake. Even their poisonous relative does not really resemble them. When sautéed they taste like fine beef. Living in Erieville despite the losses, offered unexpected gems. Morels growing under the shed was one of them.

My mom, ever in search of the perfect holiday gift sent us mushroom blocks inoculated with the spores of mushrooms from garden catalogue companies. Usually, we managed to raise some to harvest. One year we went crazy and had a box of portobellos, a block of oysters, a shiitake block and one of white button mushrooms in our upstairs bathroom where it was humid when we bathed. Still, nothing is quite as enticing as the idea of a walk in the woods to pick something wild and edible.

We collected giant puffballs a few times, but never tried to cook them. When I was four or five years old, my uncle and dad brought home a pheasant, and my mom had found a giant puffball beneath an oak tree at camp. Dinner was roast pheasant, sautéed puffball steaks and wild rice that night. I was mostly concerned with having the gaudy tail feather to keep.

I had not eaten nor seen a giant puffballs in twenty years until this summer. One day by the river in the woodland of a small park where I take my dogs to walk and swim, I found some. That day I felt like a prayer had been answered. A prayer that was, in part, a longing to know that my husband had not forgotten me. From an eighth of a mile away, through the trees I saw a big white blob. I dragged my truffle-hunters-in-training through vines to discover it was a puffball the size of a basketball. Gently I dislodged the slugs who were enjoying its tender flesh, and stashed it in the car before continuing our hike.

Once home, my first resource was, as ever, *The Joy of Cooking*. Sure enough, Irma Rombauer and clan did not disappoint! I made creamy mushroom soup, adapting their recipe to make it my own. I have a new copy of *Joy*. But hidden in a kitchen cabinet is my secret first copy which is now missing both covers and is held together by a rubber band. It had been a gift from Phillip for our first Christmas together, when I was still living in my student apartment. Its pages stained and marked with indecipherable doctor's handwritten notes, I have never been able to part with it.

After simmering my soup, I sat in the living-room with a tote full of loose photographs. I rummaged through them for any picture I could find of my husband, one in particular on my mind. There. The summer before things went bad for us, we had found some puffballs in a park. I was learning photography at that time so asked him to pose with no shirt on, holding, in one shot, several shapely potatoes he had just dug, and in another erotic close-up, an enormous puffball. I smiled up at the ceiling toward the direction of heaven's possibility and said out loud, "hi, honey," as I held the picture and smelled the perfume of simmering soup.

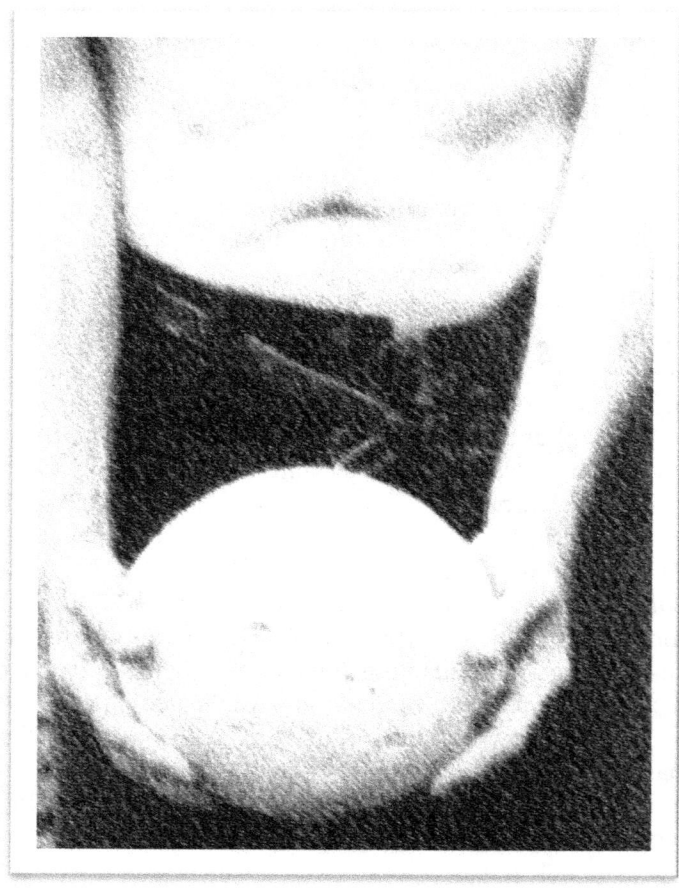

photo by Rachael Ikins © 1990

As Summer Falls Away

Rains fell in sheets, water rose
ankle high. Long slow gray day, a day
for curling with cat and book in bed.

Then, the wind.

White skies' blue
brightness blinds, wind pushes
powder-heavy banks; ragweed, goldenrod,
sedge grasses, heads nod, bow, capes swing
back, a flourish. Last bees not warmed
enough to harvest.

Hurry, autumn.

Iron-weed lace, a paradox,
echoes deeper purple. Asters open
royal lashes, gaze a final time
at September.

Next, the leaves.

Turning Point

The bowl balances
on one note that snuck in
with the darkening dawn sky.

That fills the silence of birds.
July drains away and August belongs
to the crickets and katydids,
the dusty brown grasshoppers of September.

When October teases shadows
from the edge of the woods
mesmerizing summer toward autumn.
Even as we still pretend.

Late October

Dawn wakes with its eyes closed.
Fists of wind scrub leaves' color
from naked trees. Autumn silence.

Pierced by a blue jay's warning;
chipmunks scold, voices last heard
in childhood woods where memories whispered,
that early darkness, uneasy stories of loss,
witches and winter stealth.

Then lashes flutter. Blue-eyed morning yawns,
cheeks blushed sugar-maple red. Reaches for moon's
crescent, a necklace, saunters down the path
to the lake.
into day.

Pumpkin Vines

march across the world
and one green heart swells
on a stout stem.

If I rest my cheek against this skin
it prickles.
It is warm like life,
singing the song
of sunlight.

The voice of my own heart
choruses, wow wow wow!

My toes root in the earth.
Pumpkin twines around my
ankle, holds me tight.
I go down singing, beating,
Two bodies, one heart.

Rachael's Woodland Cream Puffball Soup
Adapted from the Joy of Cooking

2 Tbsp butter or margarine
2 C puffball mushroom
2 C chicken stock
¼ C sliced onion
2 Tbsp fresh cut parsley diced finely
1 C of plain yogurt
½ tsp salt
⅛ tsp paprika
⅛ tsp ground nutmeg
3 Tbsp beer or white wine *

Melt butter in a soup pot. Having brushed the dirt off the giant puffball with a vegetable brush, cut into thick slices and then cube them until you have 2 cups or 16 ounces. Cook the pieces in the butter until they begin to turn golden brown. *They will shrink in size and do smell wonderful. A light mushroomy scent.* Add stock, onion, and parsley. Bring to a boil. Reduce heat and simmer covered for 20 mins. Remove from heat and process in blender or food processor. Return to pot and combine with 1 cup of plain yogurt. Cook but don't boil. Season with salt, paprika, nutmeg and beer. Serve with a dollop of sour cream and garnish of parsley.

*The original recipe calls for white wine. Phillip interchanged these many times, for example in cheese fondue.

Fried Puffball Mushrooms
From Livestrong.com

puffball mushroom
1C milk
1 egg
seasoned breadcrumbs
oil or butter

In one bowl beat the egg and milk together. In a second bowl have ready breadcrumbs seasoned with herbs such as thyme, oregano, rosemary from the garden. Slice the puffball into thick slices and dredge through the egg mixture, then the breadcrumbs. Have a heated skillet ready. Sauté each slice in oil or butter, using only a minimal amount of oil or butter as the puffball will absorb most of it. Drain on paper towels and serve immediately while piping hot.

Puffballs can also be used in place of tofu, cubed and added to miso soup. They can be used as a healthier alternative to meat and are a good choice for a sauce-based stir-fry or with scrambled eggs as they absorb other flavors. Once cooked puffballs can be frozen for future uses.

Raquela's Taco-stuffed Zucchini

2 medium zucchini
2 Tbsp butter
2 Tbsp chopped onion
chili powder
salt
cumin
1 egg beaten
½ cup breadcrumbs.
½ cup cheddar grated cheese.
½ cup of refried beans
½ cup sautéed ground beef.
chicken, vegetable, or beef stock
tomatoes
sliced avocado
shredded lettuce
cheddar cheese
sour cream

Preheat oven to 350°F.

Halve zucchini. Scoop out pulp leaving shells ½ inch thick. Set pulp aside. Melt butter skillet and add onion stirring until soft. Add squash pulp. Season with chili powder, salt and cumin to taste. Stir and cook until hot. Remove from heat. Add egg, breadcrumbs, cheese, refried beans, and ground beef.

Rub the squash shells with butter and fill them with the stuffing. *I like to put them in a bread pan which is the perfect size for two and keeps them from tipping over.* Pour in ⅛ inch of chicken vegetable or beef stock. Bake for 25 minutes or until squash is tender when pricked with a fork. Have ready bowls of chopped fresh tomatoes, sliced avocado, shredded lettuce, cheddar cheese and sour cream. When ready to serve, if not eating immediately, heat each in microwave for a minute or until heated and then add toppings of your choice. Crumble tostadas over the top for an extra crunch.

Rachael's Twist on Sweet Zucchini Bread
Adapted from Joy of Cooking

Preheat oven to 350°F. Grease a 9 x 5 inch loaf pan.

1 ½ cups all-purpose flour
1 tsp baking soda
1 tsp baking powder
¼ tsp cinnamon

Blend well in a large bowl:
¾ cup sugar or sweetener
2 large eggs, beaten
½ cup vegetable oil
1 tsp vanilla
½ tsp salt.
2 C grated zucchini
6 oz semi-sweet chocolate chips or chocolate chunks (half a bag)
8 oz chopped walnuts
½ C shredded coconut

Mix together in a bowl flour, baking soda, baking powder, and cinnamon. In a large bowl blend sugar, eggs, oil, vanilla and salt. Stir in the dry ingredients. Blend with a few strokes. Add zucchini, chocolate chips, walnuts, and coconut. Stir well. Bake until bread pulls away from sides of pan, about 45 mins. Test for doneness with a toothpick or fork. Cool in pan 10 mins before removing from pan to cool on a rack. This bread freezes well.

Baked Pumpkin Seeds

Pumpkin seeds
Olive oil
Sea salt

Spread fresh pumpkin seeds cleaned of the pith on a cookie sheet drizzled with olive oil. Sprinkle with sea salt. Bake on a low temp 275-300° F turning seeds often until they are a nice golden brown. Store in a sealed container.

After Halloween you can cut up and peel the unburnt remains of your jack o lanterns and cook in water until softened. Purée in blender until smooth and store in freezer bags to use for squash soups and breads.

Winter

By the time Phillip was eighty-two, I still had not had a poetry manuscript accepted for publication, even though we both worked hard at it. One day he hugged and kissed me in the kitchen in front of the sink, then looked into my eyes and said, "My life is pretty much over. I have achieved what I wanted to so it doesn't matter much to me anymore. But you, you are just beginning. I want you to make it as a poet while I am still alive to know this."

I was grief-stricken and overwhelmed with the truth of his words and this seemingly impossible wish. All our life together anything he ever wished for, if it was in my power, I accomplished it.

Phillip had been gradually succumbing to infirmities of old age, cancer, heart disease and its offshoots, one of which was dementia. We agreed that he would spend the harshest winter months in Texas reconnecting with his adult children and come home in spring. His health failed faster than either of us had expected. Phillip's daughter, who after twenty-three years of our being together, had never accepted that her father was happier in his second marriage, decided to keep us apart. After a couple months of daily phone conversations with Phillip, my calls went unanswered and letters came back 'return to sender.' As it was neither financially or physically feasible for me to travel to Texas, and no way he was physically or mentally capable of returning to central New York on his own, we were separated. He died June 1, 2010 at 10:00 p.m. in a small Texas hospital. I learned this from the lawyer I had hired to see what legal rights we had. He told me that this was a sadly common story. A caregiver taking control of a person and their social security and cutting them off from people they love. I learned that Phillip had been wheelchair bound and had lost the use of his hands. There had been no way that he could call or write to me.

Phillip had tried over the years to protect me as best as he could. We had no way of knowing that once he went to visit his children in 2007, we would never see each other again.

My mother suggested I try to call him from her house and miraculously I got through. His last words to me before the phone disconnected were, "I love you desperately."

Between his departure to Texas in 2007 and the official notice of his death in 2010, I did many odd things. Grief takes strange turns. It is intensely personal. Once I had no way to reach him and little money, I left our house, abandoned most of our animal family to a shelter, and my car—which Phillip had made sure through the bankruptcy process would remain mine as a small bit of security if he died. I literally ran. Our dachshund, Lowrider, my darling Katie, and I moved in with a friend in Albany. I was destitute and scared. I didn't know her well, but we became lovers. My understanding of what love was, having been totally defined by my intense closeness with my husband, was tested. The relationship was unhealthy, but it was all I had to cling to. The news of Phillip's death came to me in her kitchen. It took years of emotional and physical abuse before I was able to break away and leave her.

I didn't understand that some people are one-person people. I missed him so much. Through all the chaos, upheaval and loss, I had managed to save certain photographs of him and snuck secret looks at them. I continued to talk about Phillip with friends. Some of his expressions, his wacky dry jokes I still use. He did, in fact, brand my heart. He tattooed his name across it, the scar from my lobectomy as real a signature as any. I am still his after thirty-seven years. Someone once specified that he was my "late" husband. No, he is my husband. I know he died, but that does not diminish our love.

When I was a young woman, I told my mother, staring over the counter into her eyes while she made egg salad, that as far as romance was concerned, I was holding out for the Big One, the fireworks, the magic, the fairytale and happily-ever-after. It took years of suffering and numerous mistakes for me to realize that I had been blessed to have just that. While our time together was less than some couples, there were years of pure joy, and although we have been separated by circumstance and death, the love we created together lives.

His absence sneaks up on me sometimes. Anguish washes over me when I least expect it, like the day after my coffee maker had made its final pot. After consigning my mini Mr. Coffee to the trash, I brewed myself coffee in a French press and saved a cup in the fridge for later. Preoccupied with chores and animals in the afternoon I grabbed the cup to set in the microwave. Out of the blue I felt as if I had time-traveled back twenty years—Phillip and his microwaved cup of coffee every afternoon, coffee cup riding to work on the hood of his Jeep without falling off, coffee forgotten in the microwave because we became involved elsewhere. That scent. The scent of grief.

Before he passed away, I asked a friend to send him my chapbook *Slide-show* (so that it would bear her address rather than mine). I have always wondered if he received it and was able to read it. I tried my best to fulfill his request to "make it" as a poet, and while one chapbook doesn't mean you've "made it", it did contain more than one prize winning poem. I founded a poetry feature and open mic soon after the book came out – my poetry journey had begun for real, and I wished desperately for him to know it.

Since the End of It

She found his shaving brush and mug
With a round of soap behind the folded shower rug.

She ruffled the bristles.
She sniffed the soap and remembered his neck.

One Saturday 20 years ago he stopped
By between ER calls.

She led him to the bathroom.
Opened the medicine cabinet so he could see:

New mug, razor, and shaving cream.
"Last time I used that type of shaving stuff,

I was a POW in a German camp," he said,
One elbow resting in the other hand,

Fingers over his mouth. "They used straight razors
And strops." She rubbed her temples' ache, a terrible

Mistake. But later, on her shabby couch they leaned
Thigh-to-thigh. He wept. "I didn't know you wanted

Me here until I saw that shaving gear."
Afternoon sunlight descends toward dark.

She lays out one rusty blade, then the strop
And soap that scrubs her memory clean of

That walk on the Canal when her twins slid
Silently red between her legs. He rode ahead.

She wraps them in paper like you'd fold a present or a fish.
She lifts out egg-shells from the trash.

Lifts cat food can lids, an empty box of migraine pills,
Sets her wrapped package deep. Surrounds herself with dogs,

Peels wild apples for sweet sauce or a pie,
Who can say? She rubs one wrist against her forehead

Smells the faintest hint of soap.

Blizzard Magic

Windchill -30,
slantwise snow,
I grab a red scarf
to cover my face.
Head out with the dogs,
wearing my mother's old parka,
Her last, loved for its length,
covered her to the knees. I zipped
her into it weeks before she died,
her eyes blue, wide as a five year old's.

An out-of-style coat I can't seem
to part with,
her scarf wrapped
across my stuffy nose,
me, 2 weeks sick already with
this winter's virus.
Unable to smell anything.
I gasp as wind sears raw membranes,
inhale.

I smell my mother,
Revlon lipstick, Estée Lauder,
hair spray, and
a ghost of cigarette smoke.
3 winters since her death.
A wisp of smoke shadows
my shoulders. Wind playing,
Or a familiar arm?

Prelude to Winter

Coyotes ululating to half moon,
toad a fisted prayer on windowsill,
killdeers cry 'murder' in gangs,
September night wind.

Single butterfly flames out, wilding
as the year shifts down to sleep,
sinks into trees haunted
by dawn's blinking
Venus.

Winter Journeys, Reading Snow

One set of tracks twines
around a second. Their thread
spools over the field.
Night hides owls' hunt.

Dawn toes snow away, packeted
pellets of mouse parts, owl feast. 18 geese
carved from low clouds,
skid onto the pond.

Minnows arrow into leaf mast.
Ice surrenders to water under the bridge.
Birds clamber onto ice. Sun sinks
behind sky's gray satin. Winter silence.

We trudge home, hearts thrum and panting.
Voices call, pin our ears, sky choreography angles
toward sunset.

Wingbeats wash a beach of broken twig,
ripples fan, ice scrim too thin to have held their bodies,
but it did.

Polar Vortex

January

almost gone.
Buried in feet of snow.
Wolf moon looking through
a caul of horizontal flakes,
lashed by wind driven from
the Pacific across the plains.
Squirrels show before sunrise
when it is -5.

January's

weight creaks
the bones of the house.
Presses an implacable hand,
scribbles a fingernail, message
on the inner sides
of the kitchen windows
in frost, "I can take you.
Any time I want."

The New Year : March

Laddered branches lean
against Night's wall
Sky fills with returning birds.
As far as my eye can see.
Birds. Susurrus, wind, their wingbeats.
Voices; robins, starlings, grackles, redwings.
In a few months competitors.
For now cohorts.
their bodies jostle, chivvy above the black pens
of scribbling tree branch. I can almost decipher the calligraphy,
before the flocks dissolve.
Descending into woods,
calling celebration.
We are here.

The Thing is Your Life

you get caught up in the avalanche
or gravity and speed down paths
bouncing and chipping.
You accumulate dents, leave
paint flakes and broken pieces strewn
like wedding rice behind you.

Then one day the universe shifts.
The planets align or Mercury isn't in retrograde; there isn't a full moon.
You spin to a stop. Fetch up against some rock, a boulder that scrapes
skin.

After the bruises and the blood-letting,
after the sprains and torn muscles,
broken bones knit enough
to bear weight— it may not be pretty.
Scrabbling on hands and knees.
Levering yourself upright with a deadfall tree branch—

you stand. Retching and dizzy.
You look back. There is no going back.
Its all lava or flood.
So you limp forward through fog, smoke or sudden startling patches
 of too-bright light as tight as a burst wine-skin with grief.

But a berry offers itself to your parched lips.
A thrush chortles in the trees,
 and bit by bit as you inch along
tattered fragments of yourself float into your field of vision.
In the tang of berry on your tongue or the scent of camp fire smoke.
You are

here and there at once. You tie your torn jacket to make a satchel
and pick each remnant from the thorns that hold it and layer them,
soft as spider silk in your bag.

One day you won't be bleeding any more, bruises will fade,
and the bag will be shiny with fullness—
all the portions of yourself you'd thought you'd had to jettison to save
yourself. But you never stopped missing them.

One night by candle light in a cabin high up the mountain,
you will spread these pieces across a table or bed or the floor and
marvel at the god who made sure that of all the thousands, the ones you
needed most turned up here
And you put yourself back together.

Latest Winter Night: Moonrise with Dragons

Invisible fingertips patter
my face, riffle my hair, smooth my cheeks.

My eyes meet the moon's. Geese tattoo
scrawled messages across her face.
No more broken glass splinters

when I breathe in, no more knife
to the throat, all skin bundled away.
Safe to bare my hair to the wind.

Some naked white curl of me all
through winternight shriveled, waited.

Invisible fingertips patter
my face. Above me crabapple branches

pour winter-stored wine, budding
tips, new stars flash, captured fire flies.

Some naked white curl, my self
stretches, lifts away, my heart, flies

over silver with dragons, distant thunder,
their voices fill my ears. All of us remember.
We are the message: suddenly, spring.

Invocation

Low pink light.
Scarf-draped lamp,
you sigh, push sheet,
blanket aside. 3 a.m.

You collect my legs' fret,
ankles, feet in your lap.
One strong thumb circles
ball of my left foot on
the heart-line—sure enough,
wild flounder starts to slow.

Your other palm cups my heel;
a morsel, delicacy or a baby's head.
Fingers stroke my arch. Your music
lulls confused tympanies.

"Close your eyes."

Once you held my heart in your hand.
Once you told me my heart beats for both
when yours fluttered, a captive bird crazed
to escape. We owned each other.

Quiet voice 5 a.m. I sleep.
I dream you are alive.

Rachael's Goulash for Convalescents

I invented this dish after a severe bout of flu. It was the first thing that tasted good to me. It can be spiced up for those who are healthy.

1 C rice
½ lb. lean ground beef, turkey, or chicken (or tofu for vegans)
salt
pepper
1 small zucchini, shredded
1 can diced or stewed tomatoes
Parmesan or cheddar cheese

Make a cup of rice. *I like brown rice. For convenience, the boil-in-a-bag kind is great.* While the rice is cooking:

Shred zucchini with a cheese grater.
Sauté about a half lb. of lean ground beef, ground turkey or ground chicken. Season lightly with salt and pepper.
In a large frying pan combine meat and zucchini shreds. Stir and cook for a few minutes until the squash is heated through. Add tomatoes. Heat.
Remove from heat. Pour finished rice into the rest of the mixture. Sprinkle with Parmesan cheese or some shredded cheddar before serving. Enjoy and get well soon.

Rachael's Winter Garden Goulash Casserole

Ground beef, chicken or turkey
Pasta macaroni or orzo
1 bag frozen Roma tomato sauce
1 bag frozen spaghetti sauce w herbs
1 bag frozen shredded zucchini
1 bag frozen pumpkin puree
1 bag frozen pattypan squash
1 bag puffball crumbles *or canned mushrooms*
2 cubes frozen basil in olive oil
Fresh cut parsley, rosemary and thyme—*dried will also work*
1 bag frozen chicken or beef stock
1 cup wine of your choice *I used Pinot Grigio, can also use beer*
Diced shallots
2 cloves garlic chopped fine

Sauté the beef until cooked through. Combine everything except the pasta or rice and the wine in a large stockpot. You can just peel bags off and put a lid on the pot. Start on low heat to defrost. Once all ingredients have thawed, remove lid and increase heat until the mixture begins to boil. Then reduce heat to simmer. Let it cook for several hours until it reduces to a thick mixture, stirring occasionally. Make sure to check it while it cooks so the bottom doesn't burn. Leave in fridge overnight to enhance flavors.

When ready to use, prepare pasta or rice as per directions on package. Choose amount depending on number of servings. While the pasta cooks, heat the goulash on low heat and add the wine or beer. Don't boil as you will lose the flavor of it. At this stage if you wish you can also add a cup of plain yogurt or low fat sour cream.

Preheat oven to 350°F
Drain finished pasta. In a greased or sprayed with Pam casserole, combine pasta and goulash. Spoon into casserole dish and top with breadcrumbs, crumbled blue tortillas, or panko crumbs –your choice. Top that with fresh shaved Romano/parmesan mixed with a handful of mozzarella. Place casserole dish on foil or baking sheet and bake for 20-25 minutes until bubbly and top is golden brown. Serve with spinach wraps, crusty French or Italian bread and salad.

Rachael's Winter Pizza

Naan mini breads, Bobolis or pizza dough
Winter goulash
Mozzarella
Parmesan

Preheat oven to 425°F

Spread about a half cup winter goulash onto Naan. Sprinkle with cheeses. Bake for 20 minutes.

Rachael's Winter Dip
Based on allrecipes.com

1 bag frozen garden spinach
1 jar pickled artichoke hearts
1 cup of Alfredo sauce *I use store-bought sauce*
4 oz. cream cheese
1 cup mozzarella
½ cup Parmesan

Preheat oven 350°F

In an 8 x 8 inch baking dish spread thawed and drained spinach, drained artichoke hearts. Pour Alfredo sauce over. Add cut up blocks of cream cheese. Sprinkle mozzarella and parmesan over. Bake for 30 minutes or until bubbly and cheese on top is golden brown. Serve with tortilla chips, torn spinach wraps, or crusty French bread.

Variation:
Spread on a mini Naan with some added cheeses and baked at 425° F for 20 minutes results in a delightful personal pizza lunch.

"What Love Looks Like" courtesy of Kip Opperman © 1984

We loved chocolate in all its many forms. Our cookbook library included many books on nothing but chocolate. I use it today even in a classic Mexican chili recipe. It is not just for dessert any more.

Obviously nothing in the following recipe grew in my garden. I include it as the winter dessert du jour for fun and in memory of the many wonderful evenings we created such delicacies as tempura fried orange sections dipped in chocolate sauce—melted over the fire, fresh fruits dipped in dark chocolate fondues, Devil's food cakes, and chocolate frostings decorated with live pansies, nasturtiums or marigolds from the garden.

Crack
Yes, it is addicting

12 oz. bag semi sweet or milk chocolate morsels
12 oz. bag white chocolate morsels
2 sticks unsalted butter
1 sleeve Saltine crackers *I have also used gluten free table crackers*
1 cup brown sugar

Line a lipped baking pan such as a jelly roll pan with foil. Preheat oven to 350°F

While oven heats, line pan with one layer of crackers. In a large saucepan melt butter and brown sugar. Cook 5 minutes until bubbly and caramelized. Pour over crackers. Bake for 15 mins.

While it bakes melt the morsels in double boiler or microwave. Remove hot cracker mixture from oven with care. Pour/spread darker chocolate layer of melted chips. Divide white morsels into separate containers and add food coloring of choice. *Ie: red and green for Christmas, blue for Hanukah, team colors and so on.* Be creative but be quick. Drop dollops of white and colored onto the chocolate already in pan. Drag a knife through to create swirling marbleized designs. Decorate with seasonal sprinkles, colored chocolate eggs, nuts, coconut etc. You can vary flavor by adding peppermint or other extract OR buy other flavors of chips such as butterscotch or sea salt caramel. Refrigerate overnight. The next day, break or cut into pieces making sure to peel all the foil off. Store in fridge in sealed container.

Because life is short, eat dessert first!

Author's note: Phillip suffered from heart disease and I have a family history of it, all recipes included in this book are heart-healthy variations. Some include gluten-free ingredients. Dietary restrictions don't mean food has to taste less than delicious. We found the restructuring of French classics into heart friendly alternatives to be an enjoyable and successful challenge.

photo by Rachael Ikins © 1994

Love Endures

In the summer 2011, my two dachshunds and my cat, Katie, and I moved into a one-bedroom apartment in suburbia. I had sold our house, and once settled, worked hard at my writing and visual arts. In the years that followed I won more prizes for both. The number of chapbooks published grew to five with the addition of three published by Finishing Line Press in Kentucky and I was getting ready to release my first fantasy novel. My artwork hung in the New York State Fair. Through Finishing Line, I received a small honorarium to attend a writer's conference at a castle in Ireland 2014. I wished as each milestone happened, that my husband and I could sit over the breakfast table and discuss all the details.

One Saturday, I collected mail from the apartment building basement where our unit's mailboxes hung in a row. An older gentleman I had seen around the complex walked down the few stairs as I was ripping open a manila envelope from Oklahoma City Community College. It contained my copy of the student-run journal *Absolute*. A painting and a photograph had been chosen as illustrations plus a poem. My painting submission titled "Shelter," a pen and ink of a mother elephant sheltering her baby with her trunk, had won Critic's Choice Award/ Best in Show. I was bursting with excitement. I introduced myself to the stranger and said, "Hi, my name is Rachael. I'm your upstairs neighbor. I'm a poet and artist. I just got news of a prize I won and the magazine with my work." I flapped my mail at him with shaking hands. "Can I show you? I never get to share the excitement with a human being. The dogs and cat really aren't moved."

He laughed and told me his name was Don. What a good sport. He accepted the proffered reading material. After pulling his glasses from a breast pocket, he was silent as he read. Then he looked up with a peculiar expression on his face. His next words shocked me.

"You aren't by any chance related to? No, you couldn't be, but the name. Are you related to Dr. Phillip Ikins?"

"Yes," I said. "He is my husband."

To which Don responded, "I loved that man."

Don turned out to be a retired operating room X-ray technician who had worked with Phillip for thirty years. We shook hands and I climbed upstairs to sit down in my living room, stunned. Phillip did know. I petted Katie and the dogs. Katie, Lowrider and I had shared his voice, his touch. A huge comfort to me. Goosebumps rose on my arms and neck. For all the self-doubt and disasters along the way, he was the only person who never stopped believing in me from the first poem he read.

Until we meet again.

Shelter ©2014 Rachael Z. Ikins

Question

The cats wake me before the sun.
I slip back toward sleep listening to them
up and down the stairs. One dog jumps off
our bed to join them.
It is still dark, just before 6 a.m.
Your back against mine a warm length, solid
and familiar. Expected.
I think, "I'm not getting up.
You can feed the cats, let dogs out." I float
closer to sleep's surface, break through,
about to tell you that and then, open my eyes.
The cats rocket off walls.
You are not here.

Every day, chores finished,
we'd ride bikes on the canal,
separate paths but keep in touch, walkie talkies.
Meet at the car later, shiny, empty of cares,
hearts humming.
We'd drive to a corner café
for coffee, savor autumn sun,
muscle fatigue,
each other,
after it all.

Once 3 heart attacks and cancer
brittled your bones; you cried at breakfast
telling me you dreamt you were able
to ride your bike again.
Your tears dripped into oatmeal. I keep trying
to write about it.

You have been gone 8 years.
So much has happened.
The portrait I painted of you hung
in several galleries, and I performed poetry voices
in front of a backdrop of my art at
a small family art school owned
by those friends who used to serve us
coffee after rides.

I own my own house. My own heart surgery,
somehow I found my way back onto my bicycle seat,
pedaling by a lake that clucks and chuckles.
On my drive home
I pass a Dunkin. Sometimes
I pull in for
a drive-through
double espresso.
Our drink of choice.

Did you ride with me,
today, back around a curve of poplars,
just out of sight?
No dream,
real as the sweating blush
of shag-bark maple leaves,
the pink spread of ivy that carpets
the woods opposite the lake?

Do you?

Dogs and Dining
by Phillip M. Ikins

Historically one is continually impressed by the presence of dogs in the salons and dining halls of the ancients, the same animals who rushed along at the hunt or simply followed and chased caravan. Their constant closeness in pictures or chronicles tells us that they were allowed in the mess in ancient times and certainly in medieval times. It was much more than companionship or amusement.

In a contemporary era, those blessed with a Newfoundland-Labrador, a rare hybrid golden retriever sired, of course, by a black and white traveling salesman, one Lhasa Apso, an ancient failing Pekingese mix named Pooh and his youthful Pekingese friend, Piglet, readily recognize the canine contribution to history. They endow the "car wash" approach to fine dining with their continual head shaking, tongue propelling, audible and visual salivation, none of which disguises in any degree their sole consuming interest in your plate or rejections from it.

There is little doubt that in times past, domesticated dogs contributed strongly to the entertainment at the time of victualing and were ever present for various other reasons. The reward of these beasts at the close of a meal or even a course was and is to consume the remains on each plate, vessel, or trencher. The utter completeness of their efforts never fails to impress.

The salivary brilliance and sheen leaves a diner or cook with the definite conviction that here is a most valuable tool with this new technology, dog involvement in kitchen processes. Indeed, we find ourselves quite loathe to place our bowls and plates in the dish washing machine. We feel sorry for our non-dog-companioned neighbors who must employ a superfluous electrified dishwasher to his or her post prandial cleaning experience only to achieve the same end.

Go back far into remote times to judge the usefulness of the dog's role in the mess. Not only was it pleasurable to the indulged animal, but his or her total absorption in the task of cleaning the trencher or consumption of bones cast beneath tables left the host with a goodly amount of his kitchen duties already accomplished to more than a minimal degree. Certainly, a better end product than the lye-based soaps and rinses of that by-gone era could possibly have provided. Soaps made of lye and ash were oily or caustic and certainly could not compete with the brilliantly polished salivary patina enhanced by the dogs. Rinsing those soaps was often relatively ineffective, time consuming, and failed to remove the taste of the smelly chemical purifier.

Of course, this was long before the time of Louis Pasteur and his novel theories on infection and sterilization, certainly before the discovery of and belief in bacteria and their certain consequences. The microscopic appearance of germs, bacteria or viruses would not have been appropriate to historic thinking of those times. The plagues and epidemics of antiquity were never remotely reasoned as related to contact or contagion.

No person could or would have judged more by eye-sight the pristine state of the dog-tongue-cleansed vessel. Satisfactorily shiny and well done. Good dogs!

Rachael Ikins has been nominated for the Pushcart Prize & CNY Book Award multiple times and won the 2018 Independent Book Award for *Just Two Girls*. She featured at the Tyler Gallery 2016, Rivers End Bookstore 2017, ArtRage gallery 2018, Caffe Lena, Saratoga Springs, *Aaduna* fundraiser 2017 Auburn, NY, Syracuse Poster Project 2015, and Palace Poetry, Syracuse. Her work is included in the 2019 anthologies *Gone Dogs* and *We Will Not Be Silenced* the latter Book Authority's #2 pick for the top 100 Best New Poetry Books for 2019. She has seven chapbooks, a full length poetry collection and a novel. She is a graduate of Syracuse University and Associate Editor of Clare Songbirds Publishing House. She lives in a small house with her animal family surrounded by nature and is never without a book in hand.

www.ingramcontent.com/pod-product-compliance
Lightning Source LLC
Chambersburg PA
CBHW052112110526
44592CB00013B/1578